Copyright © 2024 Octavian Investments

All rights reserved

The characters and events portrayed in this book are fictitious. Any similarity to real persons, living or dead, is coincidental and not intended by the author.

No part of this book may be reproduced, or stored in a retrieval system, or transmitted in any form or by any means, electronic, mechanical, photocopying, recording, or otherwise, without express written permission of the publisher.

ISBN-13: 9781234567890
ISBN-10: 1477123456

Cover design by: Art Painter
Library of Congress Control Number: 2018675309
Printed in the United States of America

CONTENTS

Copyright	
THE PAX ROMANA METHOD	1
Ancient Lessons for Modern Business Survival	2
A Note Before We Begin	4
PART I	6
Chapter 1: The Fall of the Roman Republic -- Or, Everything Was Fine Until It Wasn't	7
How Rome Got Into This Mess	8
The Lessons for Your Business	10
Chapter 2: The Rise of Augustus -- What a 19-Year-Old Can Teach Us About Business Strategy	12
The Advantage of Having a Clear Vision	13
Decisive Action in Uncertain Conditions	15
Modern Leaders Who Got This Right	17
Chapter 3: Winning Underdogs -- Why Being Smaller Is Sometimes the Actual Advantage	19
David Understood Leverage Before Business Schools Taught It	20
Scipio Africanus and the Art of Reframing the Fight	21
The Modern Underdogs Who Changed the Rules	22
On Resilience	24

PART II — 25

Chapter 4: Step 1 -- Online Presence and Branding — 26
- Your Website: Stop Treating It Like a Brochure — 27
- Brand Identity: What You Consistently Communicate — 29
- The Sales Funnel: The Road From Stranger to Client — 31
- Social Media: Be Intentional or Be Invisible — 33

Chapter 5: Step 2 -- The Offers — 35
- The Signature Offer: What You Are Known For — 36
- Entry-Point Offers: Lower the First Step — 37
- Recurring Revenue: The Floor Your Business Stands On — 38
- On Pricing — 40
- Thirty Ideas for Recurring and Digital Revenue — 42

Chapter 6: Step 3 -- The Customer Experience — 45
- The Feeling Your Brand Is Committed to Creating — 46
- The Client Journey: Mapping Every Vote — 47
- Onboarding: The First Impression That Actually Counts — 48
- When Things Go Wrong: The Moment That Defines the Relationship — 50
- Offboarding: Designing the Ending — 52

Chapter 7: Step 4 -- Systems, Automation, and Operations — 53
- Standard Operating Procedures: The Language of a Scalable Business — 55
- Automation: Let the Machine Handle the Machine Work — 57
- Turning Services into Products: The Scalability Shift — 59
- Website Assistants and AI: The New Front Desk — 61
- The Delegation Model — 63

Chapter 8: What Great Businesses Actually Have in Common -- A Field Guide — 64
- They Know Exactly Who They Serve — 65

They Have an Offer Architecture That Makes Sense	66
They Deliver an Experience Worth Talking About	67
They Run on Systems, Not Heroics	68
They Think Long and Move Quickly	69
PART III	70
Chapter 8: When Rome Fell -- Understanding Business Distress Before It Becomes Business Failure	71
The Early Signals Most Business Owners Miss	73
The Cost of Waiting	74
Chapter 9: Turning Around a Distressed Business Using the Pax Romana Method	75
Diagnose Honestly	76
Cut Strategically	77
Rebuild Revenue With What You Have	78
Stabilize First, Then Build	79
PART IV	80
Chapter 10: Turning Crisis Into Opportunity	81
The Mindset That Finds the Opening	82
Practical Strategies for Finding Your Opening	84
The Long-Term Lesson	86
Chapter 11: Building a Legacy	87
Defining What You Stand For	88
Culture: The Invisible Operating System	89
Giving Back as a Business Strategy	90
Planning for What Comes After You	92
PART V	94
Chapter 12: Introducing Octavian Investments	95
Who We Are and How We Work	96
The Gold Rush Method	97

The Growth Ecosystem	98
The Pax Romana Resilience System	99
Where You Fit Right Now	100
Our Offer Stack	101
PART VI	103
Chapter 13: My Story -- From a 17-Page Document to Building an Empire	104
Quick Reference: The Pax Romana Method at a Glance	107
Pillar One: Online Presence and Brand	108
Pillar Two: The Offers	109
Pillar Three: The Customer Experience	110
Pillar Four: Systems and Operations	111
Using This Framework as an Ongoing Diagnostic	112
Conclusion: Your Pax Romana	113
Where to Start	115
What Building Actually Looks Like	117
A Final Word on Why This Matters	118
About Andrea Oliver	120

THE PAX ROMANA METHOD

ANCIENT LESSONS FOR MODERN BUSINESS SURVIVAL

Andrea Oliver
Founder, Octavian Investments

Copyright 2024 Octavian Investments LLC and Andrea Oliver

For every business owner who has ever felt like they were building the plane while flying it.

You are not as far behind as you think.

A NOTE BEFORE WE BEGIN

Let me be upfront about something: I did not write this book to impress you.

I wrote it because I kept having the same conversation over and over. A business owner -- smart, capable, clearly working hard -- sitting across from me and saying some version of the same thing. "I know what I should be doing. I just cannot seem to actually do it." Or: "I have taken the courses. I have read the books. I am still stuck."

That gap between knowing and doing is the most expensive real estate in business. It costs people years. It costs them revenue. Sometimes it costs them the whole thing.

This book is my attempt to close that gap. Not with more theory. Not with a framework so elegant it belongs in a Harvard Business Review article but falls apart the moment you try to apply it on a Tuesday when your biggest client is unhappy and your bookkeeper just quit. I want to give you something you can actually use.

The Pax Romana Method is built around four things: your brand and online presence, your offers, your customer experience, and your systems and operations. It is designed to be implemented in the real world, by real people running real businesses, under real constraints. The chapters ahead will tell you what to do, in what order, and why. The only thing you have to bring is the willingness to actually do it.

I should tell you something about how I got here, because context matters. I am not a consultant who studied business from the outside and then started telling people what to do with theirs. I built my consulting practice the same way a lot of you built your businesses: accidentally, out of necessity, by figuring it out as I went, and by making enough mistakes to eventually understand what actually works.

The document that started it all was 17 pages long. I wrote it to capture a process I had developed, sold it for $500, and watched it outperform programs ten times its size and five times its price. That experience taught me something I have never forgotten: people do not need more information. They need clarity about what to do next, delivered in a way they can act on immediately.

Everything I have built since that document has been a refinement of that principle. Implementation over information. Always.

Now, about the Roman thing. I know. Bear with me. History is one of the most useful business tools that almost no one is using -- not because history is a perfect map for modern problems, but because human beings have been running organizations, managing resources, navigating competition, and trying to build something that lasts for a very long time. The patterns repeat. The failures repeat. And the things that worked -- actually, durably worked -- turn out to be remarkably consistent across centuries.

The Pax Romana is one of those things. The period of stability that Augustus created out of chaos is a masterclass in systematic thinking, long-term vision, and the kind of unglamorous foundational work that actually holds an organization together under pressure. It is also, frankly, a great story. And great stories make concepts stick.

So. Let us go back in time for a minute, and then bring it all forward to your business, your clients, your revenue, and your freedom. Let us get to work.

PART I
The Lessons of Pax Romana

CHAPTER 1: THE FALL OF THE ROMAN REPUBLIC -- OR, EVERYTHING WAS FINE UNTIL IT WASN'T

I want to start with a confession: the first time I read deeply about the fall of the Roman Republic, my immediate reaction was not "how fascinating." It was "oh no, this is my client list."

The parallels are a little too accurate for comfort. A system that worked brilliantly for decades, slowly undermined by complexity it was never designed to handle. Leadership that was supposed to serve the whole but gradually became more focused on self-preservation. Resources stretched across too many fronts. A population of citizens, of employees, of customers that was increasingly exhausted and increasingly skeptical.

Rome did not collapse because Romans were bad at running things. Rome collapsed because the systems that had built the Republic were not designed for the scale the Republic eventually reached. And when the cracks appeared, the people in charge responded with short-term patches instead of structural repairs, until the patches stopped holding.

If that sounds like any business you know, you are paying attention.

HOW ROME GOT INTO THIS MESS

The Roman Republic at its height was a genuinely impressive system of governance. For its era, it was sophisticated, checks-and-balances-driven, and expansive in who it allowed to participate in civic life. It built an empire stretching from the British Isles to the edge of Persia. Its roads, aqueducts, and legal frameworks were engineering and institutional achievements that the world would not see matched for another thousand years.

The trouble with building a very large, very successful empire is that it creates a very large, very tempting pool of wealth and power. And wealth and power, left to human nature without strong accountability structures, tend to concentrate. Senators who were supposed to represent the people started representing themselves. Generals who were supposed to serve the state started building personal armies. Taxes that were supposed to fund infrastructure started funding corruption.

Sound familiar? Not because history is damning, but because human incentives are remarkably consistent across time. When there is no clear accountability for how power is used, people use it for themselves. This is not cynicism. It is a design principle worth building around.

The Gracchi brothers tried to fix the inequality problem through land reform. They were killed for it, establishing the cheerful precedent that reformers could be silenced by the people most threatened by reform. After that, things escalated from dysfunction to outright chaos. Civil wars became routine. Julius Caesar crossed the Rubicon, got himself declared dictator for life, and was assassinated before the ink was dry on the title. His death triggered another round of civil wars. By the time Octavian arrived on the scene, the average Roman was exhausted, broke, and deeply skeptical that anyone in charge was actually interested in making things better.

That is your market, by the way. Exhausted. Skeptical. Looking for someone who is actually going to deliver.

THE LESSONS FOR YOUR BUSINESS

The fall of the Roman Republic teaches three things that apply directly to running a business in difficult conditions.

First: systems that are not maintained will eventually fail. It does not matter how well they were designed originally or how well they worked in the past. A business that runs on the founder's personal relationships, institutional memory stored only in one person's head, and processes that exist nowhere except in habit is a business that is one departure away from chaos. Rome's Republic worked until it did not. Your informal systems will work until they do not. Build the real thing before you need it.

Second: short-term thinking is the most expensive thinking. Every decision Rome's late-Republic leadership made to preserve personal power in the short term accelerated the collapse of the system that gave them that power in the first place. In business, the equivalent is optimizing for this month's cash flow at the cost of the relationships, quality standards, or operational foundations that will determine next year's revenue. The patch is not the repair. Build toward the real solution even when the patch is faster.

Third: your customers are looking for stability. This was true in ancient Rome and it is true in your market right now. People will pay a premium for the confidence that you will show up, deliver what you promised, and not give them a reason to start over with someone else. Trust is not a soft metric. It is a revenue driver. Build it into everything you do.

The business owner who reads this and thinks "my business is not remotely like the fall of Rome" is probably right about the specifics. The one who reads it and thinks "but a few of those dynamics feel familiar" is the one who will get the most out of the chapters ahead.

CHAPTER 2: THE RISE OF AUGUSTUS -- WHAT A 19-YEAR-OLD CAN TEACH US ABOUT BUSINESS STRATEGY

When Octavian arrived on the Roman political scene, nobody was particularly impressed. He was 18 years old when Caesar was assassinated. He had no battle experience, no established political base, and was competing for the future of Rome against Mark Antony, who was a decorated general, a seasoned politician, and a man with a very large army at his disposal.

The general consensus among Rome's power brokers was that Octavian was not really a threat. He was a kid. An heir on paper, but nothing more than that.

They were wrong. And the reason they were wrong is the most important business lesson in this entire book.

THE ADVANTAGE OF HAVING A CLEAR VISION

Octavian understood something his opponents did not. He was not just trying to win a power struggle. He was trying to build a system that would make power struggles irrelevant. His competitors were playing a chess match. He was redesigning the board.

Where Antony and others wanted to inherit Rome's power, Octavian wanted to rebuild Rome's institutions. He spent years after the civil wars were won systematically creating the structures that would allow the empire to function without constant intervention from the top. Tax reform. Military professionalization. Legal standardization. Infrastructure investment. Communication systems. The whole thing.

Not glamorous work. Not the stuff of great drama. But extraordinarily effective.

The Pax Romana -- the roughly two centuries of relative peace and stability that followed -- was not an accident. It was the direct result of an 18-year-old who decided that winning was not enough, that what he was building needed to outlast him.

How many business owners do you know who think that way? How many are so focused on getting through the quarter that the idea of designing something to outlast them has not crossed their mind in years? We get so deep inside the daily operation that the longer view disappears entirely. Augustus never let it disappear.

ANDREA OLIVER

That discipline is what separated him from everyone else who was competing for the same prize.

DECISIVE ACTION IN UNCERTAIN CONDITIONS

Here is the other thing Augustus did that most people struggle to replicate: he made decisions in the fog.

One of the most paralyzing things about running a business is that you almost never have complete information. You have partial data, best estimates, educated guesses, and a nagging feeling that you are missing something important. Waiting for certainty before acting is, in practice, choosing not to act. The world does not pause while you gather more data.

Octavian formed the Second Triumvirate with Antony and Lepidus, knowing it was a temporary alliance of convenience. He helped crush their mutual enemies, secured his position, and then systematically dismantled the alliance when the moment was right. He did not wait for a perfect moment. He created conditions and moved into them.

In business, this looks like launching the offer before the website is perfect. Starting the outreach campaign before you have exactly the right messaging. Hiring the team member before the role description is fully defined. None of those things are reckless if you are moving with clear intent toward a clear outcome. The risk of waiting is almost always higher than the risk of moving imperfectly.

I have watched business owners talk about a launch for two years and never launch. I have watched others launch something imperfect and refine it into something excellent over six months. The people who launched are further ahead every single time. The people who waited are still talking about it.

MODERN LEADERS WHO GOT THIS RIGHT

Howard Schultz came back to Starbucks in 2008 when the company was in serious trouble. He did not just cut costs and hope for recovery. He closed hundreds of stores, retrained the entire workforce on the core product, rebuilt the brand's identity around the experience rather than the transaction, and invested in digital infrastructure at a moment when most executives were cutting everything non-essential. Within two years, Starbucks was not just recovering. It was outperforming its pre-crisis numbers. He had a vision and he moved toward it with the kind of decisive, sometimes uncomfortable action that vision requires.

Reed Hastings at Netflix made one of the most controversial decisions in recent business history when he pivoted from DVD rentals to streaming. The short-term backlash was severe. Customers complained loudly. The stock dropped. Analysts questioned his judgment publicly. He had seen where media consumption was going and he moved toward it while others stood still. Netflix did not just survive the disruption. It became the disruption that others had to survive.

Indra Nooyi at PepsiCo looked at shifting consumer preferences before anyone was talking about them at the boardroom level and started repositioning a legacy brand around health and sustainability. Not because it was the easy or immediately profitable path, but because the data showed where the market was heading. She played the long game and the long game paid out. Under her leadership, PepsiCo grew revenues by more than 80 percent.

None of these people had perfect information when they acted. All of them had a clear vision and the willingness to commit to it before the results were guaranteed. That combination is what distinguishes the businesses that lead from the businesses that follow.

CHAPTER 3: WINNING UNDERDOGS -- WHY BEING SMALLER IS SOMETIMES THE ACTUAL ADVANTAGE

I want to tell you something the big players in your industry would prefer you not to believe: being smaller is frequently an advantage. Not a consolation prize. Not something to eventually overcome. An actual, genuine, structural advantage -- if you know how to use it.

The businesses I admire most are the ones that stopped trying to be smaller versions of their largest competitor and started being the best version of themselves. That sounds like a bumper sticker. It is also a business strategy that works with remarkable consistency across industries and eras.

DAVID UNDERSTOOD LEVERAGE BEFORE BUSINESS SCHOOLS TAUGHT IT

The David and Goliath story gets told as a story about faith and courage. That is fine as far as it goes. But it is also a story about leverage, which is considerably more useful for our purposes.

David did not go up against Goliath and try to win a hand-to-hand combat match. He changed the terms of engagement entirely. He used a weapon he was genuinely expert with, at a range where Goliath's advantages were completely irrelevant. Goliath's strength, his armor, his experience in close combat -- none of it mattered at forty yards with a sling. The battle Goliath came prepared to fight never happened. David changed what the battle was about.

In business, your Goliath is whoever in your market has more resources, more brand recognition, more established relationships, more marketing budget. Trying to beat them by doing the same things they do, just with less budget, is a losing strategy. The way you win is by identifying the range at which their advantages are irrelevant. The problem they have decided is too small to solve. The customer they have determined is not worth serving. The channel they have ignored. The speed at which they simply cannot move. Go there. Set up shop there. Win there.

SCIPIO AFRICANUS AND THE ART OF REFRAMING THE FIGHT

Scipio Africanus is one of the most instructive military strategists in history for exactly the reason that his most famous victory was not won on the ground his opponent had chosen. Hannibal was extraordinary. His crossing of the Alps with war elephants is still studied as an example of audacious strategic thinking. He defeated Roman forces repeatedly in Italy and for a period seemed genuinely unstoppable.

Scipio's response was not to find a better way to fight Hannibal in Italy. It was to change what the war was about. He took the conflict to North Africa, threatening Carthage directly, forcing Hannibal to abandon his Italian campaign and come home to defend his own city. The decisive battle was then fought on Scipio's terms, in a context that disadvantaged everything Hannibal had spent years building.

The lesson for business is this: when you are outmatched in the competition as currently defined, redefine the competition. Change the channel. Change the customer segment. Change the delivery model. Change the problem you are solving. Do not accept your larger competitor's definition of the market as the only possible definition.

THE MODERN UNDERDOGS WHO CHANGED THE RULES

Warby Parker looked at an eyeglass market controlled by a handful of large companies charging $300 or more for glasses that cost a fraction of that to manufacture, and decided to sell direct, online, at $95, with a free home try-on program that solved the obvious objection. They did not try to compete on Luxottica's terms. They made Luxottica's distribution model the problem and their own the solution. They became a $3 billion company.

Mailchimp started as a side project and spent years being ignored by enterprise email marketing platforms. Those platforms competed on features and enterprise contracts. Mailchimp competed on accessibility. They made it possible for a florist or a yoga studio or a regional contractor to run professional email marketing without a marketing department. Their freemium launch in 2009 built the foundation of a business that sold for $12 billion. They won by going where Goliath had not bothered to look.

Basecamp competed in a market full of increasingly complex project management software by going in exactly the opposite direction. While competitors added features, Basecamp removed them. They built something deliberately simple and defended that simplicity as a design philosophy. Their customers were not the people who needed the most features. They were the people who were drowning in features and needed something that would actually get used. Owning that specific, underserved segment produced a highly profitable, long-running business that has never needed outside funding.

In every case the story is the same. You do not need to be the biggest, most funded, or most established player. You need to be clearest about who you serve, what specific problem you solve, and why your approach is better than the alternative for that person with that problem. Everything else is execution.

ON RESILIENCE

Sara Blakely got rejected by every manufacturer she approached when she was trying to produce Spanx. Every single one. She kept going not because she had unlimited optimism or particularly enjoyed rejection, but because she had conviction about the problem and confidence that the solution was real. That combination of conviction and persistence is available to any business owner reading this book. It does not require special resources. It requires a decision to keep moving.

The thing that underdogs have, almost without exception, is the willingness to take calculated risks that incumbents cannot or will not take. Large businesses have sunk costs to protect, cultures resistant to change, stakeholders to satisfy, and quarterly earnings to manage. They often cannot move even when they can see they should. That immobility is your opportunity. Be grateful for it. Use it.

PART II
The Pax Romana Method for Business Growth

CHAPTER 4: STEP 1 -- ONLINE PRESENCE AND BRANDING

The Romans built their roads for a very specific reason. They understood that an empire you cannot reach is an empire you cannot govern, trade with, or defend. The roads were not an amenity. They were the fundamental infrastructure upon which everything else depended. Trade moved on the roads. Messages moved on the roads. Armies moved on the roads. Without the roads, Rome was just a city. With them, Rome was a world.

Your digital presence is that infrastructure for your business. Not a nice-to-have. Not something to get around to eventually. The system of roads that determines whether anyone can reach you at all -- and what they find when they do.

I hear a version of the same objection fairly regularly. "I get most of my business through referrals, so I do not really need a strong online presence." And my response every time is: your referrals are checking your website before they call you. Every single one. In 2024, that is how trust is verified. The website is not where you win the relationship. It is where you confirm that winning it was the right call.

YOUR WEBSITE: STOP TREATING IT LIKE A BROCHURE

A brochure is a thing you hand someone to describe what you do. A website should be a thing that converts curious strangers into engaged prospects. These are different functions, and designing one to do the job of the other is one of the most common and most expensive mistakes in small business marketing.

When someone lands on your website, you have roughly eight seconds before they decide whether to stay or leave. Eight seconds. In that window, they are not reading your copy carefully. They are scanning. They are forming a gut-level impression. They are asking, unconsciously and instantly: Does this feel like someone I would trust with my money? Can I quickly understand what these people actually do? Is this relevant to my situation?

If the answer to any of those questions is no, they leave. And they almost never come back. This is not a theory. This is what the data on web behavior shows consistently across industries and markets.

Your website needs to do a small number of things exceptionally well. It needs to make an immediate strong visual impression that communicates professionalism and credibility. It needs to clearly explain who you serve and what problem you solve, in plain language, in the first ten seconds. It needs to build trust through evidence: testimonials, case studies, results, recognizable clients, anything that tells a visitor that someone else trusted you and it worked out for them. And it needs a single, clear call to action that tells people exactly what to do next.

That call to action should be one thing. Not five. Not a dropdown menu of possibilities. One clear path from curious to committed. The more options you give people at a decision point, the less likely they are to take any of them. This has been studied extensively. Choose the most important action you want visitors to take and make that the obvious next step.

A practical note on mobile: over half of all web traffic now comes from mobile devices, and Google's ranking algorithm prioritizes mobile performance. If your site looks great on a desktop and falls apart on a phone, you are invisible to a significant portion of your potential market and actively penalized in search results. Check your site on your phone right now. Actually do it. The results will tell you a great deal.

BRAND IDENTITY: WHAT YOU CONSISTENTLY COMMUNICATE

Brand is not your logo. I want to be very clear about this because the conflation of logo with brand is one of the most persistent and most expensive misunderstandings in small business marketing. Your logo is one element of your brand. Your brand is the totality of the impression you create across every touchpoint your business has with the world.

Your brand is your website design. It is also your proposal template, your email signature, the way your phone gets answered, the tone of your invoice reminders, the photography you choose for social media, the words you use to describe what you do, and the response time that people have come to expect from you. All of it, together, creates an impression. And that impression either builds trust or erodes it, consistently, over time.

The single most important word in brand strategy is consistency. Not novelty. Not cleverness. Consistency. Trust is built through repetition, and repetition requires consistency. When your brand sounds and looks different every time someone encounters it, people cannot form a reliable mental model of who you are. When it is consistent, recognition becomes automatic. Automatic recognition becomes the foundation of trust. Trust becomes the foundation of revenue.

The businesses that feel premium and established -- the ones where you look at the website or the proposal and think "these people clearly know what they are doing" -- have almost always made deliberate decisions about their visual and verbal identity and held to them across every execution. Decide what your brand communicates. Document it. Apply it everywhere. Do not deviate from it because you are bored with it. Your audience has seen it far less than you have.

At Octavian, our brand system is built on navy, bronze, and cream. Cormorant Garamond and Cinzel for typography. A tone that is direct, strategic, and without filler. Those choices signal something specific: strategic, established, and worth your investment. Every element was chosen to communicate to exactly the client we want to attract. Your brand choices should do the same work.

THE SALES FUNNEL: THE ROAD FROM STRANGER TO CLIENT

A sales funnel is the sequence of steps that moves someone from first awareness of your business to an actual purchasing decision. Most small businesses have a top of their funnel -- people discover them somehow, through referral or search or social media -- and a bottom, where the actual client conversation happens. What they are missing is everything in between: the steps that move interest into consideration, and consideration into a decision to reach out.

That middle section is where most sales are won or lost. A prospect who found you two weeks ago and has not heard anything from you since is a prospect who has been quietly evaluating your competitors. A prospect who has received something genuinely useful from you in the days between first contact and decision is a prospect who is already in a relationship with you before the sales conversation begins. Those two conversations go very differently.

Lead magnets and email sequences exist to build that middle section. Not to flood people with content they did not ask for, but to deliver genuine value at the moments between discovery and decision, so that by the time someone reaches out, they already feel like they know you and already believe you can help them. The sales call becomes a confirmation of a decision that was mostly already made.

Build the middle of your funnel. Decide what your version of the bridge between discovery and decision looks like. Then build it once and let it run. This is one of the highest-leverage investments you can make in your marketing, because it works continuously without requiring your personal time for every interaction.

SOCIAL MEDIA: BE INTENTIONAL OR BE INVISIBLE

Social media for business has one job: to build enough trust and familiarity that the right people feel ready to take the next step with you. Not to go viral. Not to grow a following for its own sake. Not to perform relevance for an audience that will never buy from you. To build trust with the specific people who could become your clients.

For most business owners working with other business owners, LinkedIn is the highest-leverage platform available. It is the one place in social media where professional credibility is the currency, where demonstrating expertise is expected rather than presumptuous, and where your ideal clients are actually looking for what you offer. Start there before anywhere else.

Consistency is more important than volume. Three thoughtful, genuinely useful posts per week, every week, for a year, will build more trust and more visibility than daily posts that burn you out after six weeks and go silent. The algorithm rewards consistency. Your audience rewards consistency. And your own sustainability rewards a pace you can actually maintain.

Show your thinking. Show your expertise. Show your process. Show results your clients are getting. Answer the questions your best prospects are already asking themselves in the small hours of the morning. Be the person in their feed who consistently makes them smarter or more capable in the area where you work. That is the social media strategy that actually builds a business, rather than just an audience.

CHAPTER 5: STEP 2 -- THE OFFERS

Rome's economy at its height was a sophisticated, multi-layered system. Trade came in from across the known world. Tax revenue flowed from every province. Domestic industries ran alongside imported goods. No single source of revenue was the whole picture, which meant no single disruption could bring the whole thing down.

Your offer architecture needs to work on the same principle. A business that runs on one product, one service, or one major client is not a diversified business. It is a single point of failure with overhead. The moment that product becomes obsolete, that service falls out of demand, or that client finds a better option, you are starting from zero. With overhead. Build multiple streams.

THE SIGNATURE OFFER: WHAT YOU ARE KNOWN FOR

Your signature offer is the core of your business identity. It is what, when someone describes what you do to a friend who needs you, they lead with. It should represent your deepest expertise, solve a specific and verifiable problem, and be priced to reflect the value of the result it produces rather than the hours it takes to produce it.

A strong signature offer is not your broadest offer. It is your sharpest. The thing where you can look a client in the eye and say: if you do this with me, something specific will change. Not "we will work together on some things." Something specific will change, and I can tell you what it is before we start.

That specificity is what allows you to price it properly. Vague promises command commodity prices. Specific, credible outcomes command premium prices. The work of sharpening your signature offer is the work of getting clear enough on your process and your results that you can promise something real. Most service businesses have not done that work. The ones that have are the ones commanding the prices they deserve.

ENTRY-POINT OFFERS: LOWER THE FIRST STEP

An entry-point offer is a lower-risk, lower-commitment way for someone to experience your value before deciding to invest in the full relationship. It reduces friction dramatically. It builds trust through demonstrated expertise rather than promised expertise. And it works as a qualification mechanism: people who invest even a small amount of money or time to access an entry-point offer are significantly more likely to convert to a larger engagement than cold prospects who receive a direct pitch for your main service.

The Pax Romana Resilience Blueprint is Octavian's entry-point offer. At $995, it gives a business owner a comprehensive diagnostic of where their business stands in our three frameworks, what the gaps are, and what to prioritize. It is a complete, standalone deliverable with real and immediate value. It is not a loss leader or a teaser. It is a real result.

And yes, it naturally leads to a deeper conversation. Not because we engineer it that way artificially, but because someone who has just seen a clear, honest picture of exactly what is working and what is not in their business generally wants to know what to do about it. We are well-positioned to help with that. That positioning is not accidental.

RECURRING REVENUE: THE FLOOR YOUR BUSINESS STANDS ON

If there is one shift that transforms a business from precarious to stable, it is the addition of predictable recurring revenue. Not necessarily because recurring revenue is always more profitable than project-based work in any given month, but because it fundamentally changes the experience of running the business.

When every month starts at zero, you are perpetually in pursuit mode. Every conversation is a potential lifeline. The pressure is constant. Cash flow is unpredictable in ways that make planning nearly impossible. When you have a reliable base of recurring revenue, you know what you are working with before the month begins. You can plan. You can invest. You can make decisions based on a real financial picture rather than your best hope.

Recurring revenue takes different forms. A monthly membership like the Gilded Path at $97 per month. A retainer for ongoing services. A subscription product. A licensing arrangement. The vehicle matters less than the principle: find where you are delivering ongoing value and create a structure that captures that value reliably and repeatedly.

Look at your current client relationships. Where are you doing repeat work without a formal arrangement? Where are clients coming back month after month for something they could simply agree upfront to receive on a recurring basis? Those are your most immediate conversion opportunities. Have that conversation.

ON PRICING

Pricing is a positioning statement, not just a number. When you underprice your work, you signal two things simultaneously: that the work is not particularly valuable, and that you do not believe it is. Both signals are received by your market whether you intend to send them or not. Prospects who might have been very serious buyers look at a low price and wonder what they are missing, because surely something this good cannot be this inexpensive.

I spent years pricing my own work below its value because I was afraid of losing potential clients to a number they might balk at. What I eventually understood is that the clients I was trying not to lose by discounting were frequently not the clients I actually wanted to be working with. The clients I actually wanted were evaluating me on entirely different criteria. They were asking: does this person understand my situation? Do they have a track record of results? Do I trust them? Price was secondary to those questions, and often irrelevant once the answers were yes.

Price your work for the result it produces, not the time it takes to produce it. If you solve a problem that costs a client $200,000 per year in lost revenue or inefficiency, and you do it in forty hours, the value of your work is not forty hours multiplied by your hourly rate. It is a meaningful fraction of the $200,000 problem you solved. The market will support pricing that reflects genuine value. Most small businesses charge less than the market would bear because they price from a cost or time basis rather than a value basis.

Raising your prices is also one of the most reliable ways to improve the quality of your client relationships. Higher-priced engagements attract clients who are serious about investing in solutions, who treat the process as a partnership, and who implement what they are given. Lower-priced engagements frequently attract clients who are price-sensitive because they are not fully committed, who engage halfway, and who produce worse results as a result -- which is bad for your case studies and bad for your energy. Price for the client you want. That client exists and they are looking for you.

THIRTY IDEAS FOR RECURRING AND DIGITAL REVENUE

The following list is not prescriptive. It is a set of prompts to help you identify where in your own business there is recurring value waiting to be packaged and captured systematically.

- Monthly strategy or coaching sessions structured as a flat retainer
- A membership community with exclusive frameworks, tools, and direct access
- A standalone diagnostic or assessment product priced and sold independently
- A group mastermind program at a monthly or quarterly subscription rate
- A premium email newsletter with genuine, implementable content each issue
- Digital templates: proposals, SOPs, contracts, email sequences, onboarding materials
- An online course or workshop series with recurring enrollment
- A certification program built around your proprietary methodology
- A done-with-you service retainer delivering consistent monthly output
- Quarterly business reviews structured as a subscription

- A private community with weekly live Q and A access to you
- An industry-specific resource library updated and expanded monthly
- An accountability or implementation program with structured weekly check-ins
- Monthly expert roundtable or panel sessions for your client community
- White-label frameworks or content licensed to other professionals in your field
- A monthly financial or cash flow review subscription for small businesses
- Done-for-you content delivered on a reliable monthly retainer
- Social media management as a structured monthly service
- Quarterly market intelligence reports specific to your client industry
- An annual business audit delivered as a recurring yearly engagement
- A monthly operational toolkit or system refresh subscription
- HR or hiring kit subscriptions for businesses in growth mode
- A fractional leadership service at a monthly flat retainer rate
- Email marketing management priced and scoped as a monthly engagement
- A personal or professional development curriculum delivered monthly
- Virtual assistant services at a predictable monthly rate
- A technology advisory and management retainer
- A brand asset subscription with updated templates delivered monthly
- Vendor or supplier negotiation as an ongoing advisory subscription
- A legal or compliance document subscription for small business owners

ANDREA OLIVER

The underlying principle is the same in every case: identify where you already create value on a recurring basis, then create a vehicle that captures that value reliably. The product very often already exists. You just have not packaged it.

CHAPTER 6: STEP 3 -- THE CUSTOMER EXPERIENCE

There is a concept in behavioral economics called the peak-end rule. Research by Daniel Kahneman found that people do not experience or remember an experience as the average of all its moments. They remember it primarily by how it felt at its most intense point and how it felt when it ended. Everything in between is largely averaged out and then forgotten.

This has enormous practical implications for how you design your client experience. The middle of an engagement, the weeks of work and deliverables and meetings and revisions, is where most of your energy goes. But in terms of what your client will actually remember, and therefore what they will tell other people, what matters most is the peak moment and the ending.

Most businesses under-invest dramatically in both. The onboarding is an afterthought or does not exist. The offboarding is nonexistent. Memorable peak moments happen by accident when they happen at all. Then business owners wonder why referrals are not flowing at the rate the quality of their work should produce.

Design the peaks intentionally. Design the ending intentionally. The middle will generally take care of itself.

THE FEELING YOUR BRAND IS COMMITTED TO CREATING

Before you can design an experience intentionally, you need to know what feeling you are designing toward. Not a vague "we want people to feel good about working with us." A specific emotional outcome that is both authentic to your brand and genuinely valuable to the people you serve.

At Octavian, the feeling we are committed to is clarity. Our clients come to us because their business feels chaotic, stuck, or overwhelming. The experience we create, from the first diagnostic forward, is designed to feel like someone turned on the lights. Organized. Direct. Specific. No filler. Every touchpoint in the client journey is designed to produce and reinforce that specific feeling. When a client leaves an interaction with Octavian feeling clearer than when they arrived, we have done our job.

Apple makes people feel creative and sophisticated. Zappos makes people feel genuinely cared for in a way that surprises them with its sincerity. Disney makes people feel temporarily inside a world where everything is handled and magic is possible. None of these are accidents. They are design choices applied consistently across decades. What is the specific feeling you want people to carry away from every interaction with your business? Name it precisely. Then audit every touchpoint in your client journey for whether it produces that feeling or works against it.

THE CLIENT JOURNEY: MAPPING EVERY VOTE

Think of every interaction between your business and a client as a vote. A vote for the impression you want to create, or a vote against it. The response time on an email is a vote. The clarity of your onboarding documentation is a vote. The professionalism of your invoice is a vote. The follow-up message after an engagement ends is a vote. The way your phone is answered is a vote.

Individual votes are small. But votes accumulate into a verdict. And the verdict is what your client carries into every conversation they have about you with the people they know. Their referrals are downstream of that verdict.

Map your actual client journey, not the one you intend. Start from the moment someone first hears about you and trace every step through to the last interaction after an engagement closes. At each step, note what actually happens -- not what should happen, what does. Ask: What does this communicate? Is it consistent with the impression I am trying to create? What would this feel like to someone experiencing it for the first time?

You will find gaps. Several of them, probably. That is the point. The gaps are not failures. They are opportunities your competition has not bothered to look for. Closing them is among the highest-leverage investments available in your business.

ONBOARDING: THE FIRST IMPRESSION THAT ACTUALLY COUNTS

There are two first impressions in any client relationship. The pre-sales first impression, produced by your website, your content, your proposals, and your reputation. And the post-purchase first impression: the onboarding experience.

The onboarding experience is where the promise your brand has made meets the reality of working with you. It is the moment when all the trust your marketing has built either gets validated or starts to erode. A disorganized, slow, or nonexistent onboarding process communicates something very specific: that the experience of being your client will be as disorganized as this.

An excellent onboarding experience communicates something equally specific: that you have done this before, that you know exactly what happens next, and that their investment was a good decision. It validates the choice before the real work has even started. That psychological relief has a value that is difficult to overstate.

Your onboarding should answer every question a new client is likely to have without them having to ask. What happens next? What do they need to prepare? When will they hear from you and through what channel? What should they expect, and by when?

Answer all of it proactively, in a format that is easy to follow. The result is a client who feels confident and prepared rather than uncertain and anxious, and who is therefore significantly easier to work with from the beginning.

WHEN THINGS GO WRONG: THE MOMENT THAT DEFINES THE RELATIONSHIP

How you handle problems is more powerful for client loyalty than how you handle success. When everything goes smoothly, clients are satisfied. When something goes wrong and you handle it with accountability, speed, and genuine care, clients are impressed. There is a meaningful difference between those two outcomes.

Satisfied clients continue. Impressed clients advocate. The distinction is worth designing for.

The anatomy of an excellent problem response is straightforward. Acknowledge what happened without defensiveness or excessive explanation. Take clear ownership. Communicate exactly what you are doing to address it and by when. Then address it faster than you committed to. That sequence, done consistently, builds the kind of trust that no amount of smooth delivery can create on its own, because you have proven something rare: that you can be trusted when things are hard.

The businesses that lose clients over problems are almost never the ones that had the problem. They are the ones that responded to the problem poorly. You can control how you respond. Control it intentionally.

OFFBOARDING: DESIGNING THE ENDING

Most businesses have no offboarding process at all. The engagement ends, both parties move on, and the relationship quietly evaporates. Given everything we know about the peak-end rule, this is the single most avoidable and most consequential gap in most client experiences.

A thoughtful offboarding process does several valuable things at once. It gives the client a clear sense of closure and accomplishment, making the value of the engagement feel concrete and real rather than abstract. It reinforces the relationship at exactly the moment when the regular interaction is ending, ensuring that the "end" feeling they take away is warm and complete rather than abrupt. And it creates a natural, zero-awkwardness moment to ask for a testimonial, a referral, or a conversation about what comes next.

The investment is small. A final summary of what was accomplished and what changed. A check-in message thirty days after the engagement closes. A relevant resource sent at a natural follow-up moment. A brief note when you see something in the market that is relevant to their business. Small gestures. Disproportionately memorable, because almost nobody else is making them.

CHAPTER 7: STEP 4 -- SYSTEMS, AUTOMATION, AND OPERATIONS

Let me paint a picture that I suspect will feel familiar.

It is 7pm on a Tuesday. You have been at it since 7am. You are behind on three things that were supposed to be done yesterday. Your inbox has unread messages you know require real responses. You have a proposal to finish, a client question to answer, and a recurring task you cannot remember whether someone handled last week. And somewhere in the background, there is a strategy you were going to work on once you had time to think.

You have not had time to think.

If that picture looks familiar, the problem is not that you work in a difficult industry or that you are managing too many things. The problem is that you do not have systems. You are personally holding together the operational fabric of your business, and the business can only operate as long as you are personally holding it. That is not a business. That is a very expensive and demanding job that you happen to own.

Augustus did not govern the Roman Empire personally. He governed through systems. Standardized law, provincial administration, professional military structures, communication infrastructure that spanned thousands of miles. The empire ran because the systems ran. The emperor's personal capacity was not the ceiling on the empire's functioning. The systems were, and the systems were designed to be far larger than any one person could manage directly.

That is what we are building in this chapter for your business.

STANDARD OPERATING PROCEDURES: THE LANGUAGE OF A SCALABLE BUSINESS

An SOP is a documented, step-by-step process for a repeatable task. The practical definition is: the thing that allows someone other than you to do something the right way, consistently, without asking you every time it comes up.

If you have not written SOPs for your core business processes, you have a significant operational fragility that you may not fully feel yet. You will feel it the first time you try to hire someone, the first time you try to delegate meaningfully, the first time you try to scale, or the first time you try to take a real vacation and discover that the business does not function in your absence.

Think about what it costs every time a task has to be explained again. Every time the same question gets asked again. Every time an execution varies because there was no standard to execute against. Now think about what it costs when that task fails -- when it gets done incorrectly -- and you spend time fixing it instead of building. SOPs are not bureaucracy. They are the precondition for getting your time back.

Start by documenting your five highest-frequency, most consequential processes. How does a new lead get followed up with? How does a new client get onboarded? How does a project move through its stages? How does an invoice get created, sent, and followed up on? How does a complaint or issue get escalated and resolved? Write each one down as if writing for someone who has never worked in your business, because someday you will need to hand it to exactly that person.

Vague SOPs are documentation theater. They look like process and function as confusion. Be specific enough that a capable person with no institutional knowledge could follow the document and get the right result. That specificity is what makes the document actually useful rather than merely reassuring to look at in a binder.

AUTOMATION: LET THE MACHINE HANDLE THE MACHINE WORK

Here is the correct sequence for automation: document the process, then automate the parts that do not require human judgment. The sequence matters. Automating a broken or undocumented process just makes the mess run faster and more consistently. Get the system right first, then automate the right system.

The highest-leverage automation opportunities for most small and mid-sized businesses are predictable. Lead capture and follow-up: when someone inquires or opts in, an automated sequence should run to acknowledge, deliver any promised resource, and initiate the next step without requiring anyone to remember to do it manually. Appointment scheduling: tools like Calendly or the scheduling function inside Go High Level eliminate the back-and-forth of finding a mutual time entirely. Client communication: appointment reminders, project milestone notifications, routine updates, and check-in messages should be triggered by events and timelines rather than by someone remembering to send them. Invoicing and payment: generate, send, and follow up on invoices systematically and without manual intervention, so payment never gets delayed because someone forgot to send the reminder.

None of these automation tools are particularly expensive. The businesses that are not using them are paying far more than the tool cost in lost time, inconsistent execution, and the mental overhead of holding the system together manually. Calculate that cost honestly before deciding the tools are not worth it.

TURNING SERVICES INTO PRODUCTS: THE SCALABILITY SHIFT

The majority of service businesses operate in a time-for-money model. You sell your time. Your revenue is therefore capped by the amount of time you have available. And when you are not actively working, you are not actively earning. That model has a ceiling. You will hit it, and hitting it is not a success problem. It is a structural problem that success exposed.

Productization is the process of taking the expertise behind a service and packaging it into a defined, repeatable deliverable with a defined scope, a defined timeline, and a fixed price. You are not doing less work. You are doing it in a way that creates repeatability, trainability, and eventually scalability.

The Pax Romana Resilience Blueprint is a productized service. It is a diagnostic that requires genuine expertise and judgment to deliver well. But it is structured as a product: clear inputs from the client, a defined process we follow consistently, a specific deliverable at the end, a fixed price. I can deliver it consistently, efficiently, and at a predictable quality level regardless of what else is happening in the business. I am not reinventing the approach for each client. I am applying a refined, documented process and improving it over time.

Look at your most common service engagements. What is the core transformation you produce? What is the process you follow to produce it, even if you have never written it down? Can that process be named, scoped, and offered as a defined deliverable with a fixed price? If yes, you have the foundation of a product. Name it. Define it. Put it on your website. That is productization, and it changes the economic model of your business fundamentally.

WEBSITE ASSISTANTS AND AI: THE NEW FRONT DESK

There is a category of operational problem that used to require either a full-time employee or an accepted limitation: responding to inquiries outside business hours, qualifying leads before they reach your calendar, and delivering consistent information without variability. AI-powered website assistants now solve all three simultaneously.

When configured correctly, a website assistant can answer common questions about your services, qualify incoming leads by gathering relevant context, direct people to the appropriate resources or offer, and book appointments -- at any hour, without human involvement, and without variation in quality or information.

The prospect who visits your website at 9pm on a Sunday and gets a helpful, knowledgeable, on-brand response immediately, then books a call before they go to bed, was previously a missed opportunity. They would have left your site, found someone else who was easier to engage with immediately, and never come back. Now they are booked on your calendar. That difference, multiplied across every off-hours inquiry your business receives, is a meaningful revenue impact.

The key is training the assistant to reflect your brand voice and to handle the specific questions your actual prospects ask. A generic chatbot that deflects everything to a contact form is not a website assistant. It is an expensive wall that frustrates people who were trying to give you their business. Build it to actually help, and it will.

THE DELEGATION MODEL

Systems and automation create the conditions for effective delegation. When your processes are documented, your tools are configured, and the standards are defined, you can hand off execution without losing quality. The standard lives in the system, not in your head.

Most business owners try to delegate before doing any of that foundational work. They hand someone a task with a vague description and an unstated expectation, and then they are frustrated when the result does not match their mental picture. That frustration is valid but usually misplaced. The failure is a systems failure, not a people failure. Without a clear standard to execute against, a capable person will simply do their best interpretation of what was asked. Their interpretation will frequently differ from yours.

Get the system right. Define the standard. Then delegate with clarity, with appropriate authority, and with real accountability. Review and improve the system as you learn what needs refinement. That is the cycle that actually produces reliable delegation, rather than the continuous return of work to your desk that most business owners experience.

CHAPTER 8: WHAT GREAT BUSINESSES ACTUALLY HAVE IN COMMON -- A FIELD GUIDE

I have had the privilege of working with a wide range of businesses over the years, across industries, at different stages, in different market conditions. And while every business is genuinely different in its specifics, the ones that grow consistently and compound their advantages over time share a remarkably consistent set of characteristics. Not personality traits or founder qualities. Structural characteristics. Things that were built, not inherited.

I want to walk through them here, because understanding what durable business success actually looks like in practice is the fastest way to identify where the gap is in your own.

THEY KNOW EXACTLY WHO THEY SERVE

The businesses that grow consistently have made a choice that most businesses resist making: they have gotten specific about who their ideal client is, and they have designed everything around serving that person exceptionally well. Not everyone. Not anyone who can pay. A specific person with a specific problem in a specific context, for whom their offer is genuinely the right solution.

That specificity feels risky from the inside. You are drawing a boundary. You are saying implicitly that some potential clients are not yours. That feels like leaving money on the table when you are a small business trying to grow.

The reality is the opposite. Specificity is a magnet. When a potential client encounters a business that clearly understands their exact situation, speaks their language, addresses their exact concerns, and has a track record with people like them, the decision to engage becomes dramatically easier. Generalist businesses make everyone do the work of figuring out whether the service is relevant to them. Specific businesses make that work unnecessary, because the relevance is self-evident.

The businesses that try to serve everyone end up reaching no one particularly well. The businesses that commit to serving a specific someone become the obvious choice for that someone and the first referral that someone's network reaches for.

THEY HAVE AN OFFER ARCHITECTURE THAT MAKES SENSE

Durable businesses do not sell one thing. They have a structured set of offers that serve clients at different stages of the relationship and different levels of investment. An entry point that is accessible and delivers quick, tangible value. A core offer that represents their deepest expertise and commands the pricing that expertise deserves. Recurring revenue structures that create a predictable foundation. And often a premium or intensive offer for clients who want maximum access and maximum speed.

That architecture is not accidental. It is designed. And it is designed to serve two purposes simultaneously: to make it easy for the right clients to enter the relationship at whatever level is appropriate for them right now, and to create a natural path for that relationship to deepen over time.

Most small businesses have one offer, or several offers that were developed reactively in response to client requests rather than proactively as part of a deliberate system. The result is an offer stack that is incoherent from the outside -- hard to understand, hard to choose between, and hard to build a referral conversation around. Build the architecture deliberately. Make the path from stranger to long-term client obvious and easy to walk.

THEY DELIVER AN EXPERIENCE WORTH TALKING ABOUT

Every business claims to provide excellent service. The ones that actually do look different from the outside: they have referral rates that are materially higher than their competitors, they have client relationships that last longer, and they have a word-of-mouth network that consistently brings the right new clients to their door without the cost of paid acquisition.

The difference between excellent service and service worth talking about is usually not the quality of the core deliverable. It is the quality of the surrounding experience: the clarity of the onboarding, the proactiveness of the communication, the speed and grace of the problem response, and the thoughtfulness of the offboarding. Those surrounding elements are where most businesses underinvest and where the greatest differentiation opportunities exist.

Service worth talking about is service that surprises people. Not dramatically or expensively, but in small ways that communicate genuine care and attention. The follow-up that arrived before they thought to ask for it. The resource that was relevant and useful even though it was outside the scope of the engagement. The personal note at the right moment. These are not large investments. They are large signals.

THEY RUN ON SYSTEMS, NOT HEROICS

The businesses that scale sustainably have documented their core processes, automated the parts that do not require human judgment, and built teams that can execute without the founder in the room for every decision. The businesses that plateau or burn out have not done this work and are personally holding together the operational fabric of everything they have built.

The transition from heroics to systems is uncomfortable, because it requires letting go of the direct control that most founders find natural and even comforting. Doing things yourself is faster in the short term. It is slower, more expensive, and more limiting in every term beyond the short one.

Systems create the conditions for scale. They also create the conditions for actual rest, for strategic thinking, for the kind of long-term work that heroics-mode never has room for. Build the systems not because you are ready to step back, but because the systems are what will make the business worth stepping into more fully.

THEY THINK LONG AND MOVE QUICKLY

The best businesses I have worked with have an interesting combination of qualities that are not always associated with each other: they hold a very clear long-term vision, and they move very quickly in the short term. They are not paralyzed by the question of whether a short-term action fits perfectly with a five-year plan. They move quickly, learn from what they learn, and adjust without drama.

This combination produces an organization that is adaptive without being reactive, and strategic without being slow. It is not a personality trait. It is a practice. Practice making decisions with the information you have rather than waiting for certainty that will not arrive. Practice reviewing what you learn and adjusting course deliberately. Practice maintaining the long view even as you manage the short one. Over time, these practices become the operating rhythm of the organization.

PART III
Crisis Survival

CHAPTER 8: WHEN ROME FELL -- UNDERSTANDING BUSINESS DISTRESS BEFORE IT BECOMES BUSINESS FAILURE

The Western Roman Empire did not collapse in a day. By the time the last emperor was deposed in 476 AD, the process had been underway for the better part of two centuries. The infrastructure had been neglected. The military had been diluted by mercenaries with limited loyalty to what they were defending. The currency had been debased to near worthlessness. Political leadership had become a revolving door of short-tenured emperors, many of whom reached the throne through assassination and left the same way.

Rome's fall was not a surprise to anyone paying close attention. It was the conclusion of a long sequence of compounding decisions, each of which made the next crisis slightly more likely and slightly harder to manage. At multiple points along that decline, different choices could have changed the outcome. The choices were not made. And the rest is, quite literally, history.

Business distress follows the same pattern. It is almost never a sudden, unpredictable catastrophe. It is almost always a slow accumulation of unresolved problems: a revenue stream quietly declining, margins quietly thinning, a key relationship quietly deteriorating, systems quietly failing under weight they were never designed to carry. The moment of crisis is simply the point at which the accumulation becomes undeniable and urgent rather than uncomfortable and ignorable.

THE EARLY SIGNALS MOST BUSINESS OWNERS MISS

Distress has early signals that are easy to rationalize. Revenue that used to be predictable becoming lumpy. Client relationships that used to feel solid going quieter. New business that used to arrive at a reliable rate slowing without a clear explanation. Team members who used to be engaged starting to check out. Cash that used to sit comfortably in the account starting to feel thin before the month ends.

Any one of these can have a benign explanation on any given day. Several of them together, sustained over multiple months, warrant honest and urgent attention. The question is not whether you can construct a plausible innocent explanation for each individual signal. The question is what the pattern means, and whether the pattern has been present long enough to constitute a trend.

The businesses that survive distress are almost always the ones that caught the signals early enough to have real options. The businesses that do not survive are almost always the ones that waited until the crisis was undeniable, at which point the options were severely limited.

THE COST OF WAITING

One of the most consistent patterns I have observed in my work with distressed businesses is the gap between when the owner first knew something was genuinely wrong and when they first took meaningful action. That gap is almost always larger than it should be. And the primary cost of waiting is not that the problem got bigger, though it usually did. The primary cost is that the options available shrank dramatically.

A business with six months of runway has real options and the time to exercise them thoughtfully. A business with six weeks of runway has very few options and no time for anything except crisis response. The earlier you address a problem, the more uncomfortable it feels to address it, because the emergency has not yet fully arrived. You are doing the hard work of fixing something that does not yet look completely broken. That discomfort is the price of having real choices. Pay it willingly.

CHAPTER 9: TURNING AROUND A DISTRESSED BUSINESS USING THE PAX ROMANA METHOD

The best thing I can tell any business owner in genuine distress is this: it is not over until you decide it is. I have worked with companies that were months from insolvency and returned to profitability within a year. The common factor in every successful turnaround I have been part of was not favorable external conditions. The conditions were almost always unfavorable. The common factor was the willingness to face the actual problem without flinching, make the hard decisions without delay, and execute a clear plan without being pulled back toward the familiar patterns that created the distress to begin with.

DIAGNOSE HONESTLY

The first and most important step in a turnaround is an honest diagnosis. Not the story you have been telling yourself about why things are difficult. The actual data about what is happening and why it is happening.

Pull every financial statement. Go line by line, not summary level. Where is money coming in? What are the real margins on each revenue line? Where is money going, and is each expense producing a measurable return? What does cash flow look like at 30, 60, and 90 days out? What obligations are coming due and what is the coverage?

Then go further into the non-financial signals. What is your client retention rate? What is your sales conversion rate? What is your team's actual engagement level? Where are the operational failures happening repeatedly? What do clients say when they leave, or when they quietly stop coming back without saying anything at all?

Most business owners in distress already have a clear intuition about the core problem. They are hoping the data will not confirm it, or that something will improve on its own and make the difficult conversation unnecessary. It almost never does. Name the actual problem explicitly. Write it down in plain language. That specificity is the foundation of being able to address it.

CUT STRATEGICALLY

The instinct in distress is to cut everything and cut it fast. That instinct is understandable and often counterproductive. Panic cutting -- eliminating costs without clarity about what they are actually producing -- is one of the most reliable ways to make a distressed business's situation materially worse.

Conduct a genuine line-by-line expense audit. For every line, ask: is this producing a measurable return? Is there a less expensive alternative that delivers the same result? Is this something the business actually needs right now, or something we added during a more comfortable period and have never revisited?

Negotiate with vendors before you stop paying them. Most would rather modify terms than absorb a default. The negotiation conversation is uncomfortable. The default is catastrophic. Have the conversation early, while you still have credibility and leverage.

Protect the things that generate revenue, retain clients, and maintain delivery quality. Those are not the places to cut. They are the places to optimize and strengthen, even while cutting elsewhere. The businesses that survive distress by cutting their way through almost always cut the things that would have saved them along with the things that needed to go.

REBUILD REVENUE WITH WHAT YOU HAVE

Once cash outflow is stabilized, the priority shifts to rebuilding inflow. And in almost every business, the fastest source of meaningful new revenue is not new customers. It is existing and former customers.

Reach out personally. Not with a mass email or a promotional campaign. With a direct, specific message to people who already know you, already trust you, and already have experience with what you deliver. Tell them specifically what you have available. Ask directly whether there is something you can help them with. Create a time-limited offer compelling enough to move quickly. Introduce a recurring service structure that converts a past relationship into ongoing revenue.

The economics are clear. Converting an existing or former client costs a fraction of what it costs to acquire a new one. They have already cleared the trust hurdle. They already know you deliver. Every business in distress has a list of past clients who had a positive experience and could be reactivated. Working that list before spending anything on acquisition is almost always the right sequence.

STABILIZE FIRST, THEN BUILD

A turnaround has two distinct phases, and the mistake most distressed businesses make is conflating them. Phase one is stabilization: stopping the financial bleeding, restoring cash flow to a manageable baseline, creating enough breathing room to think with some degree of clarity. Phase two is rebuilding: applying the full Pax Romana Method to create the stronger, more resilient version of the business.

Trying to do both simultaneously almost always means doing neither well. Stabilization requires focus, speed, and a narrow set of priorities. Rebuilding requires strategy, patience, and a broader view. They are different operational modes. Recognize which one you are in, commit to it fully, and transition deliberately when the time is right.

PART IV
Fortifying and Future-Proofing Your Business

CHAPTER 10: TURNING CRISIS INTO OPPORTUNITY

Every major disruption creates a re-sorting of the market. Businesses that were rigidly attached to the way things used to work lose ground. Businesses that adapt quickly gain it -- sometimes dramatically, sometimes generationally.

The 2008 financial crisis is instructive. The companies that survived it are notable. The companies that thrived during it are extraordinary. And the companies that started during it -- Airbnb, WhatsApp, Instagram, Venmo, Uber, Slack -- built some of the most valuable businesses of the past two decades. Not despite the crisis. During it. Because disruption creates gaps in the market that incumbents are too focused on self-protection to fill. Those gaps belong to whoever moves first.

Crises do not destroy opportunity. They relocate it. Your job in any disruption is to understand where it moved and to move toward it before your competitors figure it out.

THE MINDSET THAT FINDS THE OPENING

Businesses that find opportunity in crisis have a specific cognitive discipline: they are able, even in the middle of difficulty, to maintain some portion of their attention on the question of what the disruption is making possible rather than only what it is destroying. This is harder than it sounds. When revenue is down and your team is anxious and your clients are uncertain, the cognitive pull toward problem management is enormous. Problems need managing. But reserving some fraction of your attention for the question -- what does this disruption make possible that was not possible before? -- is what separates the businesses that lead recoveries from the ones that merely survive them.

LVMH pivoted from luxury perfume to hand sanitizer early in the COVID pandemic. They used existing production infrastructure to meet urgent public need, strengthened brand perception, and generated goodwill at a moment when most luxury brands were managing existential uncertainty. They asked "what can we do with what we have right now?" and then moved on the answer fast.

Shopify became a lifeline for small businesses forced to close physical locations, enabling rapid digital pivots and expanding its own customer base dramatically. The crisis that threatened Shopify's customers was simultaneously an enormous growth catalyst for Shopify. They were positioned to help before the crisis existed. When it arrived, they moved.

Zappos doubled down on customer service during the 2008 recession when nearly everyone else was cutting. They understood that in a difficult economy, businesses that make people feel genuinely valued earn a form of loyalty that cannot be purchased. They were right, and the resulting customer retention and word-of-mouth became a case study that business schools still use.

PRACTICAL STRATEGIES FOR FINDING YOUR OPENING

When a disruption hits your market, the useful questions are specific ones. What are my clients now struggling with that they were not struggling with six months ago? What capability do I have that addresses that new problem directly? What channel has become more important that I have been underinvesting in? What competitor has become slower or weaker, and what does that open up for me?

These are not rhetorical questions. They are analytical ones. Sit down with a sheet of paper and answer them as honestly as you can. The answers will not always point to a massive strategic pivot. Sometimes they point to a conversation you need to have with an existing client about a new problem you are perfectly positioned to solve. Sometimes they point to a channel shift that is relatively low-cost and high-potential. Sometimes they point to a partnership that would have seemed unnecessary before the disruption and now makes clear sense. Follow the logic wherever it leads.

The businesses that thrive through disruption are not always the most resourced or most established. They are almost always the ones that stayed closest to their clients, listened harder during the difficulty than they did before it, and responded to what they heard with something real. Stay close. Listen carefully. Respond specifically.

THE LONG-TERM LESSON

Every significant business disruption of the past century has confirmed one thing without exception: the market comes back. Not always in the same form, not always on the same timeline, not always with the same winners. But the fundamental human demand for goods and services does not disappear. It shifts, delays, changes form. It does not disappear.

This means that businesses that use disruption periods to strengthen their foundations -- to build the systems they always needed, to sharpen the positioning that was always unclear, to deepen client relationships that were always worth deepening -- emerge into recovery with structural advantages over businesses that merely endured. The recovery rewards preparation. Use the difficult period to prepare for it, and you will enter the next chapter of your business at a different level than where you started the hard one.

CHAPTER 11: BUILDING A LEGACY

There is a meaningful distinction between building a business and building a legacy. A business generates revenue. A legacy generates meaning -- and then revenue, at a scale and with a durability that a business built purely for profit rarely achieves independently.

The businesses that endure across decades -- that accumulate the kind of reputation that becomes self-sustaining, that generate loyalty that survives a bad quarter, that attract talent and clients because of who they are rather than only what they cost -- have made a choice that purely transactional businesses have not. They decided to stand for something beyond the immediate exchange.

Patagonia has built a customer relationship closer to allegiance than preference. Customers do not just buy Patagonia. They identify with it. Ben and Jerry's customers feel they are supporting something they believe in, not just purchasing a product. Zappos customers have real, specific stories of above-and-beyond service that they tell for years. None of these are flukes. They are the result of organizations that made deliberate choices about what they stood for and then built every internal and external system around those choices.

DEFINING WHAT YOU STAND FOR

You cannot build a legacy you have not defined. Most businesses are started for practical reasons rather than a clearly articulated sense of larger purpose, and that is fine. Most great businesses were not launched with a fully formed legacy in mind. But at some point, the enduring ones made a decision about what they stood for beyond the transaction -- and that decision became a filter for everything else.

The question worth sitting with honestly is: if your business disappeared tomorrow, what would actually be missing? Not the revenue. Not the jobs, though those matter too. What would be genuinely absent from your clients' experience, your community, your industry? The answer to that question is the seed of your legacy. Plant it intentionally. Water it consistently.

CULTURE: THE INVISIBLE OPERATING SYSTEM

Culture is not a set of values on a wall. Culture is what your team actually does when no one is watching, what decisions they make when the right answer is not obvious, and what they prioritize when priorities conflict. It is the operating system of the organization, running silently in the background of every interaction and every decision at every level of the business.

Strong cultures are built by leaders who model the values they want institutionalized, who hold the line on those values even when it is expensive to do so, and who recognize and reward behavior that reflects them. Weak cultures are built by leaders who say one thing and do another, who make exceptions for the wrong reasons, and who assume that articulating the values does the work of living them. The culture will reflect which kind of leader you are, accurately and without flattery.

Your culture will outlast your specific clients, your specific team members, and your specific product line. If it is strong, it will attract and retain the people and clients who belong in it. If it is weak, it will do the opposite. Build it as deliberately as you would build any other foundational element of the business, because it is at least as important as any of them.

GIVING BACK AS A BUSINESS STRATEGY

There is a version of this conversation that sounds like corporate social responsibility boilerplate, and I want to skip past it. What I actually mean is simpler and more practical than the boilerplate version: businesses that are genuinely connected to a purpose beyond profit have access to a form of loyalty that pure transactions do not generate.

This does not require a charitable foundation or a published environmental policy. It can be as direct as the way you treat your team, the clients you choose to work with, the causes you visibly support in your community, or the standards you hold your supply chain to. The specific form matters less than the authenticity. People can tell the difference between an organization that actually stands for something and one that is performing the appearance of standing for something. The former earns loyalty. The latter earns skepticism.

Newman's Own has donated 100 percent of profits to charity since its founding. That commitment is inseparable from the brand and produces a kind of customer relationship that no marketing campaign could replicate. Ben and Jerry's has integrated social advocacy into the brand at a level that sometimes generates controversy but consistently generates the kind of passionate customer loyalty that most brands would pay anything to have. The controversy, interestingly, tends to reinforce rather than undermine the loyalty among the customers they are actually trying to reach.

Find the version of this that is authentic to who you are and what your business actually values. Then make it visible and hold to it consistently. That combination is what builds a legacy.

PLANNING FOR WHAT COMES AFTER YOU

Here is the ultimate test of whether you have built a business or an elaborate job: what happens if you are not there? Not next week. Next year. Does the business continue to function? Does it serve clients at the same standard? Does the culture hold? Does the revenue hold?

For most small business owners, the honest answer reveals that what they have built depends on their personal presence to a degree that makes it effectively non-transferable. That is not a failure. It is a starting point for an important conversation about what the business would need to be able to survive and eventually thrive without you at the center of it.

Planning for continuity requires the systems work we covered earlier -- documented processes, trained teams, defined standards. But it also requires something harder to systematize: making explicit the values, the judgment calls, the quality standards that are held even when holding them is inconvenient, and the culture that makes the business feel like itself across different people and different conditions. Those things need to be articulated and transmitted rather than assumed to pass along automatically.

Ford Motor Company has lasted more than a century. Johnson and Johnson has a credo that has guided decisions across generations of leadership and survived crises that would have destroyed organizations with less clear values. These are not accidental achievements. They are the result of deliberate choices about what the organization stood for and how those standards would be maintained regardless of who was in the leadership seat at any given moment. Make those choices consciously for your own business. Write them down. Share them with the people who will carry them forward.

PART V
Expanding Your Empire

CHAPTER 12: INTRODUCING OCTAVIAN INVESTMENTS

If you have made it this far, you are not someone who was looking for more to think about. You were looking for traction. For the specific next move. For someone to tell you not just what the problem is but what to do about it, in the right order, in a way that produces results in the actual world rather than on a slide deck.

That is what Octavian Investments is built to do. This chapter will tell you who we are, what we do, which of our frameworks applies most directly to where your business is right now, and how to take a concrete next step if you want help.

WHO WE ARE AND HOW WE WORK

Octavian Investments is a growth and development consulting firm serving founders and CEOs of small and mid-sized businesses, primarily in the $500K to $5M revenue range. We work across professional services, healthcare services, construction, real estate, staffing, logistics, and multi-location retail.

The philosophy of the firm is built on a single conviction: the gap between where most small businesses are and where they could be is not a talent or capability gap. The founders and CEOs we work with are smart, capable, and hard-working. The gap is structural. It is a systems gap, a clarity gap, and in many cases a support gap. People are doing the work without the architecture that would allow the work to compound. We provide the architecture.

We are not information merchants. We do not sell you a framework and wave goodbye. Our highest-value work happens in implementation, in the specific and concrete changes that move a business from where it is to where it is trying to go. We care about what changes in your business, not about how elegantly you can describe the framework.

THE GOLD RUSH METHOD

The Gold Rush Method is our framework for revenue generation and market positioning. It is designed for business owners whose revenue is inconsistent, unpredictable, or lower than their effort warrants -- who feel like they are leaving money on the table but are not sure exactly where to look for it, or who have strong capabilities but a weak or unclear go-to-market.

The framework addresses three questions: Where is the gold, meaning what are the highest-value opportunities in your market given your specific strengths? How do you build the infrastructure to reach that gold consistently, your offers, your marketing, your sales process? And how do you establish a market position that makes you the obvious choice for the clients you actually want?

This is the starting point for business owners who need to grow revenue with intention and repeatability, rather than hoping that the conditions that generated good months in the past will continue to generate them.

THE GROWTH ECOSYSTEM

The Growth Ecosystem is our framework for building the infrastructure of a scalable business. Where the Gold Rush Method addresses revenue, the Growth Ecosystem addresses the operational and organizational structures that determine whether the business can actually sustain and leverage that revenue without requiring you to personally hold everything together.

The framework covers brand and online presence, client experience design, team structure and delegation architecture, operational systems and automation, and financial management. It is the work of making the business function like a real, self-sustaining company rather than a very busy founder with helpers. If your business cannot function when you are unavailable for more than a few days, the Growth Ecosystem is where we need to start.

THE PAX ROMANA RESILIENCE SYSTEM

This is the framework you have spent the last several chapters with. The Pax Romana Resilience System is our method for building businesses that hold up under pressure -- that survive disruption, recover from setbacks, and maintain their performance through the kind of external volatility that is increasingly just a permanent feature of the business environment.

It covers the four pillars described in this book: online presence and brand, offers and revenue architecture, customer experience design, and systems and operations. Whether you are building from a solid foundation or rebuilding from a period of distress, this framework creates the durable infrastructure that holds everything else.

WHERE YOU FIT RIGHT NOW

Most business owners we work with fall into one of three clear situations.

If your revenue is inconsistent, unpredictable, or lower than your effort and capability should produce -- if you are not sure exactly what you are selling, to whom, through what channel, or why they should choose you over the alternatives -- the Gold Rush Method is the right starting point. Revenue clarity precedes operational optimization. There is no point building a flawless system for a business model that has not been validated.

If your revenue is solid but you are personally holding too much of the operational weight -- if the business cannot function when you are unavailable, if delegation keeps failing, if the systems that worked at a smaller scale are breaking under current demands -- the Growth Ecosystem is where we begin. The operational foundation comes before the scaling.

If you are dealing with active distress, significant market uncertainty, or the need to rebuild after a setback -- if cash flow is unstable, client retention is eroding, or the business has lost its footing -- the Pax Romana Resilience System is the starting point. Stabilization before optimization. Foundation before growth.

Many clients engage across all three frameworks over time. They are designed to work together as an integrated system. Where you start depends entirely on where your business actually is today, not where you wish it were.

OUR OFFER STACK

Our offers are designed to match the way business owners actually make decisions about investing in support. Here is how we work:

- Gilded Path Membership, $97 per month: Ongoing access to our frameworks, tools, implementation resources, and community. This is consistent support and accountability without a full consulting engagement. Many clients begin here and continue it alongside other engagements.
- Pax Romana Resilience Blueprint, $995: A comprehensive diagnostic that gives you a clear picture of exactly where your business stands in each of our three frameworks, what the gaps are, and what to prioritize first. A standalone deliverable with immediate value. Also the most natural starting point for any deeper engagement, because it creates the shared diagnostic foundation we both need to build a plan worth executing.
- Business Growth Accelerator, $10,000 for a 12-month engagement: Our flagship implementation program. We work alongside you through the full build-out of the most relevant framework for your current stage, with hands-on support, regular strategy sessions, and accountability for execution. This is where the significant transformations happen.
- Stronghold Private Sessions, $1,500 per 60-minute session: Direct access for specific, high-stakes decisions, urgent strategy questions, turnaround situations, or any moment when you need a clear answer and cannot afford to wait. No prescribed agenda beyond the question you bring.

If you are not sure where to start, the Pax Romana Resilience

Blueprint is almost always the right first step. Not because it is the lowest-priced option, but because it creates the clarity that everything else depends on. You will leave with a specific, honest picture of where your business is and what should happen first. That clarity is valuable on its own. It also makes any larger work we do together significantly more effective.

Website: https://www.octavianinvestments.com

Start with the Blueprint: https://www.octavianinvestments.com

PART VI
The Story Behind the Method

CHAPTER 13: MY STORY -- FROM A 17-PAGE DOCUMENT TO BUILDING AN EMPIRE

I want to tell you how I got here, because I think it matters. Not because my story is dramatic or exceptional. It is actually fairly ordinary in the way most real business stories are ordinary -- full of moments where the right next step was not obvious, and the path forward revealed itself primarily by taking it.

I did not set out to be a consultant. Entrepreneurship found me the way it finds a lot of people: through a combination of circumstance, necessity, and a set of skills I had accumulated that turned out to be genuinely useful once I gave them a real problem to work on. There was no grand plan at the beginning. There was a problem I needed to solve and a conviction that I could figure out how.

The thing that started everything was 17 pages long. I wrote it to capture a process I had developed, a specific systematic approach to a specific problem that was producing consistent results. I was not sure anyone would pay for it. I sold it for $500.

And then something happened that I did not expect and have been thinking about ever since: that 17-page document outperformed programs I had seen that were ten times longer, five times more expensive, and had entire teams behind them. People did not just read it. They implemented it. They got results from it. They told other people about it, who bought it and got results from it too.

I have spent a lot of time understanding why. The answer, as best I can reconstruct it, is this: the document told people exactly what to do, in exactly what order, without anything that did not directly serve that purpose. No padding. No filler. No theory included because it was interesting rather than useful. Just the process itself, cleanly and completely, written with enough specificity that someone could actually follow it.

That experience is the foundation of everything I have built since. Not the $500 in revenue. The lesson. Specificity and implementation beat breadth and information almost every single time, with almost every kind of client, in almost every kind of business. People do not need more information. They need clarity about what to do next and enough confidence to actually do it.

The path from that first document to Octavian Investments was not linear, and I would be doing you a disservice to describe it as though it were. There were programs I launched that did not land the way I had designed them to. Pivots that cost real time and real money. Seasons where I had to look honestly at what was working and be clear-eyed about what was not. I know what it feels like to look at something you have poured yourself into and wonder whether the foundation is solid or whether you have been building carefully on sand.

Those experiences are not incidental to why I do this work the way I do. They are central to it. Every framework I bring to my clients has been tested on my own business first, under real conditions with real stakes. I am not teaching from a textbook. I am working from the same ground my clients are standing on, with the same constraints, the same uncertainty, and the same requirement to build something real rather than something that merely looks real on a slide.

Octavian Investments exists because I kept seeing the same gap. Capable, committed business owners working harder than their results justified, not because they lacked talent, but because nobody had ever helped them build the systems and the strategy that would allow their talent to compound. The difference between a $500K business and a $2M business is rarely the quality of the work. It is almost always the structure around the work -- the offers, the systems, the positioning, the experience, the operational architecture. That is the gap we close.

The name is not accidental. Octavian, the man who became Augustus, who looked at a fractured system on the edge of collapse and built something that lasted for centuries, represents everything I believe about what becomes possible when clear vision meets systematic execution and the patience to build the right foundation rather than the fast one.

Your business deserves that kind of build. You have already put in the work. Let us make that work compound the way it should.

Start the conversation: https://www.octavianinvestments.com

QUICK REFERENCE: THE PAX ROMANA METHOD AT A GLANCE

The following is a condensed reference for the four pillars of the Pax Romana Method. Use it as a diagnostic tool, a planning guide, or a quick reminder of the sequence when you are deep in execution and need to reorient.

PILLAR ONE: ONLINE PRESENCE AND BRAND

The goal of Pillar One is to create a digital presence that is immediately credible, clearly positioned, and structured to move the right visitors from discovery to engagement without requiring your personal attention every time.

The website must answer three questions in the first ten seconds: who do you serve, what problem do you solve, and what should someone do next. It must be mobile-optimized, load quickly, and convert visitors through a single clear call to action rather than a menu of options. Social proof must be prominent and specific -- names, results, and context rather than generic testimonials that could apply to anyone.

Brand identity must be consistent across every touchpoint. Decide on the visual and verbal identity. Document it. Apply it everywhere. Do not vary it because you are bored with it. Your audience has seen it far less than you have, and consistency is how recognition becomes trust.

The sales funnel must have a real middle section. Something of genuine value that bridges the gap between first discovery and the sales conversation: a lead magnet, a diagnostic, a workshop, a resource that delivers a real result and naturally creates the appetite for more. Build it once and let it run.

PILLAR TWO: THE OFFERS

The goal of Pillar Two is to create an offer architecture that serves clients at multiple levels of commitment, generates predictable recurring revenue, and is priced to reflect the value of the results you produce rather than the time you spend producing them.

Every business needs a signature offer: the core, highest-expertise deliverable that defines what you do and commands premium pricing. It needs an entry-point offer: a lower-commitment way for prospects to experience your value before the full relationship, priced fairly and structured to deliver a real, standalone result. It needs recurring revenue: memberships, retainers, subscriptions, or any vehicle that creates a reliable base of predictable income. And it benefits from a premium or intensive offer for clients who want maximum access and maximum speed.

Review your pricing. Price for the result, not the time. Find the clients who can see the value and design your marketing to reach more of them, rather than lowering the price to reach the ones who cannot.

PILLAR THREE: THE CUSTOMER EXPERIENCE

The goal of Pillar Three is to create a client journey that is consistently excellent from first contact through final touchpoint, with intentional peaks that are worth talking about and an ending that leaves clients feeling complete and enthusiastic rather than abrupt and forgotten.

Name the feeling you are committed to creating. Not vaguely -- specifically. Then audit every touchpoint in the actual client journey against that feeling. Fix the gaps in order of how much damage they are doing to the experience. Build a real onboarding process that validates the client's decision before the work begins. Build a real offboarding process that makes the ending feel complete and creates a natural moment for testimonials and referrals. Design at least one moment in every engagement that is specifically intended to surprise and exceed expectations.

When things go wrong -- and they will -- handle it with speed, accountability, and genuine care. Acknowledge, own it, communicate the fix, then fix it faster than you promised. That sequence builds more trust than smooth sailing alone ever will.

PILLAR FOUR: SYSTEMS AND OPERATIONS

The goal of Pillar Four is to build an operational infrastructure that allows the business to function and grow without requiring your personal presence in every process, every decision, and every execution. The business should run because the systems run, not because you are running yourself into the ground.

Document your five highest-frequency core processes as SOPs. Write them with enough specificity that a capable person new to your business could follow them and get the right result. Identify the parts of each process that do not require human judgment and automate them: lead follow-up, appointment scheduling, client communication milestones, invoicing and payment, routine reminders. Productize your most repeatable services. Deploy AI tools on your website front end to extend your responsiveness beyond business hours. Then delegate the execution with clear standards, clear authority, and real accountability.

The sequence is: document, systematize, automate, delegate. Running that sequence in order produces results. Running it in reverse produces rework.

USING THIS FRAMEWORK AS AN ONGOING DIAGNOSTIC

The Pax Romana Method is not a one-time project. It is a living framework for the ongoing development of your business. Every quarter, run a brief diagnostic against each of the four pillars. Where has the business grown? Where has a gap opened up that was not there before? What is the one thing in each pillar that would create the most momentum over the next 90 days?

Businesses that use a consistent diagnostic framework across time develop a compound advantage over businesses that only think strategically when a crisis forces it. You are building something intended to last. Tend it with the same consistency you would give any other asset that is supposed to grow.

CONCLUSION: YOUR PAX ROMANA

Augustus did not set out to rule the world. He set out to create the conditions under which people could live, work, and build without the ground constantly shifting beneath them. The Pax Romana -- the peace of Rome -- was not peace as the absence of challenge. It was peace as the presence of structure: clear systems, reliable institutions, predictable rules, and the foundational stability that allows everything else to grow on top of it.

That is the vision behind the method you have just spent this book with. Not explosive growth for its own sake. Not an empire built on heroics and exhaustion and the founder's personal willpower holding everything together by force. A business that runs with intention, serves clients with genuine excellence, earns consistently, and gives you the freedom that was presumably somewhere in your original reasons for building it in the first place.

The four pillars of the Pax Romana Method are not complicated. Build the presence that makes the right people find you and trust you before they meet you. Create the offers that serve different needs at different levels of commitment and investment. Design the experience that makes people glad they chose you and eager to tell the people they care about. Build the systems that allow the machine to run without requiring you to be inside it every moment of every day. Those four things, done with care and consistency, produce something the vast majority of small businesses never achieve: a business that actually works the way a business is supposed to work.

ANDREA OLIVER

You have read the framework. You understand the principles. The only thing left is to apply them, and that is the part no book can do for you.

WHERE TO START

If you close this book and do nothing, it will join the long shelf of good ideas that never changed anything. I say that with no judgment, because I have been on that shelf myself, and I know exactly how easy it is to finish something genuinely useful and then return to the urgent demands of the present without ever creating space to act on it.

So let me be specific about what I would do if I were you, right now, in the next 48 hours.

First, identify the one pillar of the Pax Romana Method where the gap in your business is largest. Not where you are weakest overall -- where the gap between where you are and where you should be is creating the most drag on everything else. For most businesses, it is either the offers (revenue is inconsistent because the offer architecture is unclear) or the systems (revenue is acceptable but the operational fragility is limiting growth). Start with whichever one is true for you.

Second, name one specific thing within that pillar that you will build or improve in the next 30 days. Not a category. One thing. The sales funnel. The onboarding process. The SOP for client intake. The recurring offer structure. One specific, concrete thing with a start date and an end state you can describe clearly.

Third, put it on the calendar. Not as a vague intention. As a blocked commitment with a deadline. The difference between a plan and a wish is a calendar entry.

That is it. One pillar. One thing. One deadline. The rest of the method can follow in sequence. Momentum matters more than comprehensiveness at the start, and the first thing done well will make every subsequent thing easier to build.

WHAT BUILDING ACTUALLY LOOKS LIKE

I want to be honest with you about something: building well is not a straight line. There will be weeks where the thing you built does not work the way you designed it, where a client interaction does not match the experience you intended to create, where a system that seemed solid reveals a gap you did not anticipate. That is not failure. That is the normal texture of building something real.

The businesses I have watched grow most consistently are not the ones where everything worked the first time. They are the ones where the founder treated every gap and every failure as information rather than verdict -- as data about what needed to be refined rather than evidence that the whole endeavor was misguided. That posture, applied consistently over time, is what turns a rough first version into a refined, excellent system.

Every great business has a version of the 17-page document in its history. The early offer that was rougher than what it eventually became. The process that was manual before it was automated. The client experience that was adequate before it was exceptional. The system that held things together through sheer effort before it was properly documented and delegated. The difference between the businesses that became great and the ones that stayed mediocre is not that the great ones started with better material. It is that they kept refining.

Keep refining. The standard is not perfection on the first pass. The standard is better than last quarter, and better than that the quarter after.

A FINAL WORD ON WHY THIS MATTERS

I want to close with something that the business-building conversation does not always make room for, and that I think is worth saying clearly.

You are building something. Not just a revenue stream or a career or a professional identity. An actual thing that employs people, serves clients, creates value, and -- if you build it well -- will outlast any single difficult moment, any one difficult year, any single difficult market condition. That is not a small thing. That is the kind of thing that changes the material conditions of multiple lives, including yours.

The businesses that build well and serve well and run on solid foundations are the ones that become the stable employers in a community, the trusted partners that clients rely on across years and through transitions, the organizations that survive the disruptions that shake out the businesses that were built on less solid ground. That kind of durability has value that extends well beyond the revenue it generates.

You deserve to build something like that. The people who work for you deserve an organization built on real foundations. Your clients deserve a business that will be there for them not just this year but the year after that and the year after that.

That is what the Pax Romana Method is for. Not an abstract framework on a page. A real, usable, implementable system for building the kind of business that holds. Use it. Build the thing. And when you do, let me know.

With real respect for what you are building,

Andrea Oliver

Founder, Octavian Investments

www.octavianinvestments.com: https://www.octavianinvestments.com

ABOUT ANDREA OLIVER

Andrea Oliver is the founder of Octavian Investments, a growth and development consulting firm serving founders and CEOs of small and mid-sized businesses. Her firm's work is organized around three proprietary frameworks -- the Gold Rush Method, the Growth Ecosystem, and the Pax Romana Resilience System -- and one operating conviction: implementation beats information, every time.

Her path to consulting was anything but conventional. She began with a 17-page document sold for $500 that outperformed programs ten times its size, and that experience became the philosophical foundation of everything she has built since. The frameworks she teaches have been tested on her own business first, under real conditions and with real stakes.

Andrea works with business owners across professional services, healthcare, construction, real estate, staffing, logistics, and multi-location retail. Her clients come to her when they are done consuming information and ready to build something that actually works.

The Octavian Method is her first book.

Learn more at: https://www.octavianinvestments.com

www.ingramcontent.com/pod-product-compliance
Lightning Source LLC
Chambersburg PA
CBHW070146230526
45471CB00002B/534